# CHOOSE
# JOY

### BECAUSE HAPPINESS ISN'T ENOUGH

## KAY WARREN

**Revell**

*a division of Baker Publishing Group*
Grand Rapids, Michigan

Published by Revell
a division of Baker Publishing Group
P.O. Box 6287, Grand Rapids, MI 49516-6287
www.revellbooks.com

Printed in the United States of America

ISBN 978-0-8007-2172-5-4

14  15  16  17  18      7  6  5

# Contents

# Welcome to Choose Joy:
# Because Happiness Isn't Enough

 Have you wondered why some people seem to experience deep and authentic joy in their daily lives—even in the toughest times—and others can't seem to find it no matter how hard they search? Many of us eventually give up the pursuit, assuming we were unfortunate enough to have been standing on the wrong side of the door when God was handing out joy. It has often seemed to me that only a few lucky people receive the gift of joy and that fewer still know joy's "secret." I'm here to say, I've learned that's just not true!

Even though it may not feel that way to you at this moment, joy is available to you. You may be thinking, I don't experience joy as much as other people do. It's just not my thing. Or, joy means living in denial of all the pain in the world. But as I've discovered in my own life, joy is not about your circumstances or about how you feel. It is definitely not about living in denial and ignoring sorrow or pain. Joy is something much deeper, richer, more stable, and definitely more accessible than you might have thought. That's the beauty of the joy God offers. You no longer need to live in fear or worry, because God's joy will always be available to you. In this world you will have trouble, Jesus says. But you can still take heart. You can still receive joy. You are not dependent on anyone or anything other than God and yourself to know joy.

*Welcome*

There's one promise I want to give you as we start: I will be honest with you about my life and my search for joy. I will not gloss over my doubts, failures, and sins, and I will admit to you—and myself— my sweaty, middle-of-the-night wrestling with God over issues of faith. I find my own faith bolstered when I know someone else is struggling and sometimes succeeding in letting Christ be formed in her. Spiritual growth doesn't happen automatically and is rarely pretty; we will all be "under construction" until the day we die and we finally take hold of the "life that is truly life" (1 Tim. 6:19). So let's walk side by side for a while, and I'll share with you what I'm learning about how to choose joy every day . . . in the best and worst of times . . . in every moment.

As you go through the study, I'd love to hear from you! I hope you'll share with me, and others traveling down this road, the ways you're choosing joy and the lessons God is teaching you. At KayWarren.com you can post your own stories, find more teachings and resources, and also sign up for the free *Choose Joy* daily video devotionals. Each day you will receive an email from me with a video message that will urge you to look a little deeper at your life and challenge you to choose joy in a way you may not have expected.

Thanks for joining me as together we choose joy,

*Kay Warren*

# Choose Joy
# Study Overview

*Choose Joy* is a four-session study, designed with the flexibility to meet your group's needs. Each session is recorded in a short (25 minute) and long (45–75 minute) format. Your small group can follow along with Kay's message and use the book to note key concepts as they watch, then continue with small group discussion, meditation, and personal application using the questions in this guide. The longer version works well for small groups with longer regular meetings, or can be used as the content for a special retreat or seminar.

In between sessions, you can sign up at KayWarren.com/Devotions to receive a free daily video devotion on the material for 30 days.

## Welcome

Welcome to the first session of *Choose Joy*. If you are a newly formed group or if there are newcomers in your group, take a moment to introduce yourselves.

If you are using the shorter video format, begin your time by watching the **WELCOME VIDEO** by Kay Warren before moving into the video message for Session One.

*Watch the Video Lesson now and take notes in your outline. Refer back to the outline during your group discussion.*

# Session One
## *Jesus, Man of Joy*

Joy is the settled assurance that
God is in control of all the details
of my life; the quiet confidence
that ultimately everything is going
to be all right; and the determined
choice to praise God in all things.

*Isaiah 53:3 (NIV) He was despised and rejected by men, a man of
sorrows, and familiar with suffering.*

In his _____ , Jesus was a man of _____ .

But in his _____ , Jesus was a man of _____ .

*Luke 7:34 (PH) The Son of Man came, enjoying life.*

*Hebrews 12:2b (NKJV) Who for the joy that was set before him
endured the cross . . .*

Jesus proves to us he is a Man of Joy:

Through his _____.

> Isaiah 53:2 (CEV) *He wasn't some handsome king. Nothing about the way he looked made him attractive to us.*

Through his _____.

> Matthew 23:24 (NIV) *You strain out a gnat but swallow a camel.*

> Luke 8:16 (GW) *No one lights a lamp and hides it under a bowl or puts it under a bed.*

> Matthew 7:3, 5 (NLT) *And why worry about a speck in your friend's eye when you have a log in your own? First get rid of the log in your own eye; then you will see well enough to deal with the speck in your friend's eye.*

Through his _____.

*John 2:4 (NCV) Jesus answered, "Dear woman, why come to me?
My time has not yet come."*

*Matthew 14:31 (NIV) Immediately Jesus reached out his hand and
caught him. "You of little faith," he said, "why did you doubt?"*

*Matthew 14:16 (NIV) Jesus replied, "They do not need to go away.
You give them something to eat."*

Jesus—as someone who knew joy and sorrow—gives you
permission to seek a life of joy as well.

## For Small Group Discussion or Personal Study

Use the following questions and exercises to guide your remaining small group time, as take-home material if you are using the longer session, or for further personal study.

1. How does your new understanding of Jesus, Man of Joy, differ from what you have believed or been taught about him?

2. Where are you on the bell curve Kay mentioned?

3. How can you choose joy in the middle of life's challenges this week?

4. Meditate on the words of Matthew 1:23 (GW).

   *The virgin will become pregnant and give birth to a son, and they will name him Immanuel, which means God is with us.*

   Now, imagine Jesus (God with us), Man of Sorrow, Man of Joy, walking with you through your daily life.

   - What would he laugh with you about?

   - What would he cry with you about?

   - When would he say, "Let me hold you"?

   - When would he say, "Let's celebrate"?

6. Guided Reflections: Read Hebrews 12:2 (MSG) three times.

   *Keep your eyes on Jesus, who both began and finished this race we're in. Study how he did it. Because he never lost sight of where he was headed—that exhilarating finish in and with God—he could put up with anything along the way: cross, shame, whatever. And now he's there, in the place of honor, right alongside God.*

   - What WORD stands out to you?

   - What EMOTION do you correlate with that word?

   - Take a few minutes to write, draw, or express what you experienced from reading this verse.

## PRAYER

*God, please transform me from a woman of sorrows
to a woman of joy.*

Yahweh your God is there with

you, the warrior-Saviour. He

will rejoice over you with happy

song, he will renew you.

Job 8:21 (NJB)

## Session One — Notes

## Session One — Notes

## Welcome

Welcome to your second session of *Choose Joy*. Before you begin watching today's video, take a few minutes in your group to discuss last week's message. Think through together:

- Moments you gave yourself permission to be joyful, even in challenging circumstances.

- Scriptures you read that reminded you of Jesus as the Man of Joy.

*Watch the Video Lesson now and take notes in your outline. Refer back to the outline during your group discussion.*

# Session Two
## *Joy Is a Conviction of My Mind*

Joy is the settled assurance that
God is in control of all the details
of my life; the quiet confidence
that ultimately everything is going
to be all right; and the determined
choice to praise God in all things.

*James 1:2–4 (MSG) Consider it a sheer gift, friends, when tests and challenges come at you from all sides. You know that under pressure, your faith-life is forced into the open and shows its true colors. So don't try to get out of anything prematurely. Let it do its work so you become mature and well-developed, not deficient in any way.*

False Sources of Joy:

1.

2.

3.

4.

5.

## Our True Source of Joy: ⎯⎯⎯⎯⎯⎯⎯

*Jeremiah 2:13 (NIV) My people have committed two sins: They have forsaken me, the spring of living water, and have dug their own cisterns, broken cisterns that cannot hold water.*

*Isaiah 58:14 (NIV) Then you will find your joy in the Lord.*

*Nehemiah 8:10 (NIV) The joy of the Lord is your strength.*

*Psalm 16:11 (NIV) You will fill me with joy in your presence.*

Five Convictions that Bring Joy:

God's _____ is _____.

*Psalm 148:13 (MSG) Let them praise the name of God—it's the only Name worth praising. His radiance exceeds anything in earth and sky.*

*Psalm 16:11 (ESV) You make known to me the path of life; in your presence there is fullness of joy; at your right hand are pleasures forevermore.*

God's _____ is _____ .

*Psalm 19:8 (NIV) The precepts of the Lord are right, giving joy to the heart. The commands of the Lord are radiant, giving light to the eyes.*

*Psalm 19:8 (MSG) The life-maps of God are right, showing the way to joy.*

*Psalm 119:111 (NIV) Your statutes are my heritage forever; they are the joy of my heart.*

*Jeremiah 15:16 (NIV) When your words came, I ate them; they were my joy and my heart's delight.*

God's _____ are _____ .

*Psalm 111:2 (MSG) God's works are so great, worth a lifetime of study—endless enjoyment!*

*1 Chronicles 16:33 (NIV) Then the trees of the forest will sing, they will sing for joy before the Lord.*

*Psalm 92:4 (NIV) For you make me glad by your deeds, O Lord; I sing for joy at the works of your hands.*

God's _____ are _____ .

*Psalm 18:35 (MSG) You protect me with salvation-armor; you hold me up with a firm hand, caress me with your gentle ways.*

*Psalm 117:2 (MSG) His love has taken over our lives; God's faithful ways are eternal. Hallelujah!*

*Psalm 145:13 (NIV) The Lord is faithful to all his promises and loving toward all he has made.*

God's _____ is _____ .

*Jeremiah 29:11 (NIV) "For I know the plans I have for you,"*
*declares the Lord, "plans to prosper you and not to harm you,*
*plans to give you hope and a future."*

The basis for joy is choosing the _____ over the
_____ every time.

*2 Corinthians 4:16–18 (NIV) Therefore we do not lose heart.*
*Though outwardly we are wasting away, yet inwardly we are being*
*renewed day by day. For our light and momentary troubles are*
*achieving for us an eternal glory that far outweighs them all. So we*
*fix our eyes not on what is seen, but on what is unseen. For what is*
*seen is temporary, but what is unseen is eternal.*

## For Small Group Discussion or Personal Study:

Use the following questions and exercises to guide your remaining small group time, as take-home material if you are using the longer session, or for further personal study.

1. Which of these false sources of joy trap you:

   - PEOPLE—Do you allow the actions or reactions of others to affect your mood or self-image?

   - PLACES—Do you determine your joy by where you live or where you travel?

   - POSSESSIONS—Does your joy depend on the things you have or don't have?

   - POSITION—Is your joy tied to your education, career, stage of life, marital status?

   - PERSONALITY—Do you think joy is possible for only certain personalities?

2. To experience joy this week, what changes do you need to make in your thinking that will allow you to view your circumstances through the lens of eternity rather than the lens of the temporary?

3. Prayerfully read Psalm 119:97-104 together, perhaps in different translations, making a mental note of the benefits of choosing to trust God and his Word.

   After meditating on Psalm 119, ask God to show you if there are any specific actions you need to take as you seek to live a more joyful life. Share with your group if you can. Is there:

   - a sin to confess

   - a promise to claim

   - an attitude to change

   - a command to obey

   - an example to follow

   - an error to avoid

   - a truth to believe

   - something to praise God for

4. Guided Reflection: Read Matthew 6:21 (NLT) three times.

   *Matthew 6:21 (NLT) Wherever your treasure is, there the desires of your heart will also be.*

   • What WORD stands out to you?

   • What EMOTION do you correlate with that word?

   • Take a few minutes to write, draw or express what you experienced from reading this verse.

## PRAYER

*Father, forgive me for seeking joy in anything other than you.*
*This week I will meditate on who you are;*
*help me to get to know you better so that I will more fully*
*trust you with all that concerns me.*

Philosophy may instruct

men to be calm under their

troubles, but Christian-

ity teaches them to be joyful.

MATTHEW HENRY

## Session Two — Notes

## Session Two — Notes

## Welcome

Welcome to your third session of *Choose Joy*. Before you begin this week's session, take a few moments to share with your group how the message of *Choose Joy* has impacted your week.

- Where did you go for joy this week? What was the outcome?

- What readings of Scripture led you back to the idea of God as the source of your joy?

- What circumstances were reframed by looking at them through the lens of eternity?

*Watch the Video Lesson now and take notes in your outline. Refer back to the outline during your group discussion.*

# Session Three
## Joy Is a Condition of My Heart

*James 1:2–4 (MSG) Consider it a sheer gift, friends, when tests and challenges come at you from all sides. You know that under pressure, your faith-life is forced into the open and shows its true colors. So don't try to get out of anything prematurely. Let it do its work so you become mature and well-developed, not deficient in any way.*

*Philippians 2:14-15 (TLB) In everything you do, stay away from complaining and arguing so that no one can speak a word of blame against you. You are to live clean, innocent lives as children of God in a dark world full of people who are crooked and stubborn. Shine out among them like beacon lights.*

I Fill My Heart with Joy When:

I focus on _____ .

*Galatians 3:12, 21 (MSG) Rule-keeping does not naturally evolve into living by faith, but only perpetuates itself in more and more rule-keeping. . . . For if any kind of rule-keeping had power to create life in us, we would certainly have gotten it by this time.*

Rate yourself: On a scale of 1–10 how regularly do you experience grace in your life?

I trust God for the _____.

*Matthew 6:27–28 (MSG) Has anyone by fussing in front of the mirror ever gotten taller by so much as an inch? All this time and money wasted on fashion—do you think it makes that much difference? Instead of looking at the fashions, walk out into the fields and look at the wildflowers. They never primp or shop.*

*Matthew 6:33–34 (MSG) Steep your life in God-reality, God-initiative, God-provisions. Don't worry about missing out. You'll find all your everyday human concerns will be met. Give your entire attention to what God is doing right now, and don't get worked up about what may or may not happen tomorrow. God will help you deal with whatever hard things come up when the time comes.*

*1 Peter 5:7 (PH) You can throw the whole weight of your anxieties on him, for you are his personal concern.*

Rate yourself: On a scale of 1–10 how regularly do you trust God for the future?

I balance my _____ .

*Psalm 127:2 (GW) It is useless to work hard for the food you eat
by getting up early and going to bed late. The LORD gives food to
those he loves while they sleep.*

*Psalm 127:2 (NCV) It is no use for you to get up early and stay up
late, working for a living. The Lord gives sleep to those he loves.*

*Matthew 11:29–30 (ICB) Accept My work and learn from Me. I am
gentle and humble in spirit. And you will find rest for your souls.
The work that I ask you to accept is easy. The load I give you to
carry is not heavy.*

Rate yourself: On a scale of 1–10 how balanced is your life?

I practice _____ .

*Revelation 21:4–5 (NIV) He will wipe every tear from their eyes.
There will be no more death or mourning or crying or pain. "I am
making everything new!*

Rate yourself: On a scale of 1–10 how much contentment do you
experience in your life?

# I Fill Others with Joy When:

I _____ about them.

> *1 Corinthians 13:7 (LB) If you love someone, you will be loyal to him no matter what the cost. You will always believe in him, always expect the best of him, and always stand your ground in defending him.*

> *Proverbs 17:22 (ESV) A joyful heart is good medicine.*

Rate yourself: On a scale of 1–10 how readily do you believe the best about others?

I _____ their mistakes.

*1 Corinthians 13:5 (NIV) It [love] keeps no record of wrongs.*

*Galatians 5:15 (NIV) If you bite and devour each other, watch out or you will be destroyed by each other.*

*Luke 6:37 (MSG) Don't pick on people, jump on their failures, criticize their faults—unless, of course, you want the same treatment. Don't condemn those who are down; that hardness can boomerang. Be easy on people; you'll find life a lot easier.*

*Romans 2:1 (MSG) Every time you criticize someone, you condemn yourself. It takes one to know one. Judgmental criticism of others is a well-known way of escaping detection in your own crimes and misdemeanors.*

*Philippians 4:8 (GW) Finally, brothers and sisters, keep your thoughts on whatever is right or deserves praise: things that are true, honorable, fair, pure, acceptable, or commendable.*

Rate yourself: On a scale of 1–10 how readily do you forgive others?

I _____ with their feelings.

*Proverbs 14:10 (NLT) Each heart knows its own bitterness, and no one else can fully share its joy.*

*Galatians 6:2 (NKJV) Bear one another's burdens, and so fulfill the law of Christ.*

*John 15:12 (NKJV) This is my commandment [my law] that you love one another.*

*Ephesians 4:32 (AMP) And become useful and helpful and kind to one another, tenderhearted (compassionate, understanding, loving-hearted), forgiving one another [readily and freely], as God in Christ forgave you.*

Rate yourself: On a scale of 1–10 how easily do you empathize with others feelings?

I _____ their efforts.

*Philippians 1:5 (NCV) I thank God for the help you gave me while I preached the Good News—help you gave from the first day you believed until now.*

Rate yourself: On a scale of 1–10 how often do you applaud others' efforts?

Joy and sorrow are two

parallel tracks that run

inseparably throughout our lives.

KAY WARREN

## For Small Group Discussion or Personal Study:

Use the following questions and exercises to guide your remaining small group time, as take-home material if you are using the longer session, or for further personal study.

1. Share your ratings with the group as you identify the ways you kill joy in yourself:

   - legalism

   - worry

   - busyness/workaholism

   - perfectionism

2. Share your ratings with the group as you identify the ways you kill joy in others:

   - cynicism

   - criticism

   - selfishness

   - ingratitude

3. Share your ratings with the group on how well you fill your heart with joy right now—and choose one way to fill your heart with joy this week:

   - grace

   - trust

   - balance

   - acceptance

4. Share your ratings with the group on how well you fill others with joy right now—and choose one way to fill others' hearts with joy this week:

   - believe the best

   - forgiveness

   - compassion

   - appreciation

5.  Visualize yourself as the apostle Paul, sitting in a dark, damp Roman prison, not knowing what would happen to him next, and writing this letter to his friends in Philippi:

    *Philippians 2:14–15 (MSG) Do everything readily and cheerfully— no bickering, no second-guessing allowed! Go out into the world uncorrupted, a breath of fresh air in this squalid and polluted society. Provide people with a glimpse of good living and of the living God. Carry the light-giving Message into the night.*

    As followers of Christ, we go through the same trials as people who do not have a relationship with him. Think about a situation in your life that may seem hopeless and make it impossible to experience joy fully. How can you choose to live in such a way that a watching world will see God in you as you carry the "light-giving message into the night"?

6. Guided Reflection: Read I Thessalonians 5:16-18 (NIV) three times.

   *I Thessalonians 5:16-18 (NIV) Rejoice always, pray continually, give thanks in all circumstances; for this is God's will for you in Christ Jesus.*

   • What WORD stands out to you?

   • What EMOTION do you correlate with that word?

   • Take a few minutes to write, draw, or express what you experienced from reading this verse.

## PRAYER

*God, may I become a woman of grace and trust, a woman
who reflects your joy for others to see. It's impossible for me
to do that by myself. Go deep inside me and do your work.
Change me so that I become a woman of joy, and a woman
who builds joy in others.*

Joy is rooted in gratitude.

A grateful heart is a joyful heart;

a joyful heart is a grateful heart.

## Session Three — Notes

## Session Three — Notes

## Welcome

Welcome to your final session of *Choose Joy*. Before you begin today's session, take a few moments to share with your group how the message of *Choose Joy* has impacted your week.

- What ways did you find to build joy in yourself this week? In others?

- What readings of Scripture led you back to the idea of trusting God for your future?

- Were you more aware of others who watch how your faith impacts how you respond to trials?

*Watch the Video Lesson now and take notes in your outline. Refer back to the outline during your group discussion.*

# Session Four
## *Joy Is a Choice of My Behavior*

*Romans 5:3–5 (MSG) There's more to come: We continue to shout our praise even when we're hemmed in with troubles, because we know how troubles can develop passionate patience in us, and how that patience in turn forges the tempered steel of virtue, keeping us alert for whatever God will do next. In alert expectancy such as this, we're never left feeling shortchanged. Quite the contrary-we can't round up enough containers to hold everything God generously pours into our lives through the Holy Spirit!*

Ways to Choose Joy Daily:

_____ your life.

*Psalm 90:12 (LB) Teach us to number our days and to recognize how few they are; help us to spend them as we should.*

Practice _____.

*Colossians 4:2 (MSG) Stay alert, with your eyes wide open in gratitude.*

Rediscover _____.

*1 Timothy 6:17 (NIV) . . . Put [your] hope in God, who richly provides us with everything for our enjoyment.*

Express _____ freely.

*1 Corinthians 13:13 (MSG) Love extravagantly.*

See the _____.

*Proverbs 15:15 (GW) Every day is a terrible day for a miserable person, but a cheerful heart has a continual feast.*

*Proverbs 15:13a (NASB) A joyful heart makes a cheerful face.*

_____ joyful people.

*1 Corinthians 15:33 (NCV) Do not be fooled. Bad friends will ruin good habits.*

_____ someone's load.

*Galatians 6:10 (NIV) Therefore, as we have opportunity, let us do good to all people, especially to those who belong to the family of believers.*

*Hebrews 13:16 (NIV) And do not forget to do good and to share with others, for with such sacrifices God is pleased.*

Live in the _____.

*Ephesians 5:16 (LB) Make the most of every opportunity you have for doing good.*

*Psalm 118:24 (NIV) This is the day the LORD has made; let us rejoice and be glad in it.*

Find the _____ in the mess.

*Philippians 4:8 (MSG) Summing it all up, friends, I'd say you'll do best by filling your minds and meditating on things true, noble, reputable, authentic, compelling, gracious—the best, not the worst; the beautiful, not the ugly; things to praise, not things to curse.*

You and I were created for joy

and if we miss it we miss the

reason for our existence.

Lewis Smedes

## For Small Group Discussion or Personal Study:

Use the following questions and exercises to guide your remaining small group time, as take-home material if you are using the longer session, or for further personal study.

1. Share with the group the ways you can choose joy daily:

   - simplify your life

   - practice gratitude

   - rediscover pleasure

   - express affection freely

   - see the humor

   - befriend joyful people

   - lighten someone's load

   - live in the moment

   - find the bless in the mess

2.  Prayerfully read over Psalm 43:4A (NLT) several times as a group, and emphasize a different word each time you read it.

    *Psalm 43:4A (NLT) There I will go to the altar of God, to God—the source of all my joy.*

3.  For you to experience joy, what will it be:

    *   in spite of . . .

    *   in the middle of . . .

    *   even if . . .

4. Guided Reflection: Read Psalm 126:5 (NLT) three times.

   *Psalm 126:5 (NLT) Those who plant in tears will harvest with shouts of joy.*

   • What WORD stands out to you?

   • What EMOTION do you correlate with that word?

   • Take a few minutes to write, draw, or express what you experienced from reading this verse.

## PRAYER

*Father, I want to believe that you can replace my
mourning with dancing and I can become a woman
who feels the sadness of life but still chooses to pursue joy.
I want to live today, right now, as someone who chooses joy.
Give me strength and courage to look for
your blessings on this journey.*

*I choose joy!*

## Session Four — Notes

## ANSWER KEY

### JESUS, MAN OF JOY—SESSION ONE

In his <u>ROLE</u>, Jesus was a man of <u>SORROWS</u>. But in his <u>ESSENCE</u>, Jesus was a man of <u>JOY</u>.

Through his <u>ATTITUDES</u>

Through his <u>WORDS</u>

Through his <u>ACTIONS</u>

### JOY IS A CONVICTION OF MY MIND—SESSION TWO

<u>PEOPLE</u>

<u>PLACES</u>

<u>POSSESSIONS</u>

<u>POSITION</u>

<u>PERSONALITY</u>

Our True Source of Joy: <u>GOD</u>

God's <u>WORTH</u> is <u>INCOMPARABLE</u>.

God's <u>WORD</u> is <u>RELIABLE</u>.

God's <u>WORKS</u> are <u>AWESOME</u>.

God's <u>WAYS</u> are <u>LOVING</u>.

God's <u>WILL</u> is <u>GOOD</u>.

The basis for joy is choosing the <u>ETERNAL</u> over the <u>TEMPORARY</u> every time.

# JOY IS A CONDITION OF MY HEART—SESSION THREE

I focus on <u>GRACE</u>.

I trust God for the <u>FUTURE</u>.

I balance my <u>LIFE</u>.

I practice <u>CONTENTMENT</u>.

I <u>BELIEVE THE BEST</u> about them.

I <u>FORGIVE</u> their mistakes.

I <u>EMPATHIZE</u> with their feelings.

I <u>APPLAUD</u> their efforts.

# JOY IS A CHOICE OF MY BEHAVIOR—SESSION FOUR

<u>SIMPLIFY</u> your life.

Practice <u>GRATITUDE</u>.

Rediscover <u>PLEASURE</u>.

Express <u>AFFECTION</u> freely.

See the <u>HUMOR</u>.

<u>BEFRIEND</u> joyful people.

<u>LIGHTEN</u> someone's load.

Live in the <u>MOMENT</u>.

Find the <u>BLESS</u> in the mess.

## About Kay

**Kay Warren** cofounded Saddleback Church with her husband Rick Warren in Lake Forest, California. She is a passionate Bible teacher and respected advocate for those infected and affected by HIV and AIDS, as well as orphaned and vulnerable children. She founded Saddleback's HIV/AIDS Initiative. Kay authored *Say Yes to God* and coauthored *Foundations*, the popular systematic theology course used by churches worldwide. She has three children and five grandchildren. Learn more at **www.kaywarren.com** and follow her on Facebook (Kay Warren) and Twitter (@KayWarren1).

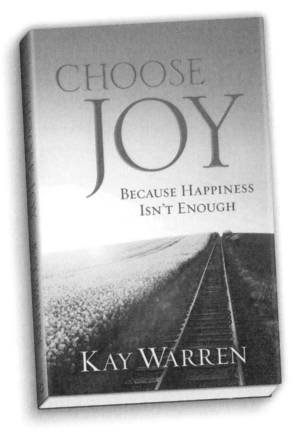

# CHOOSE JOY Devotions

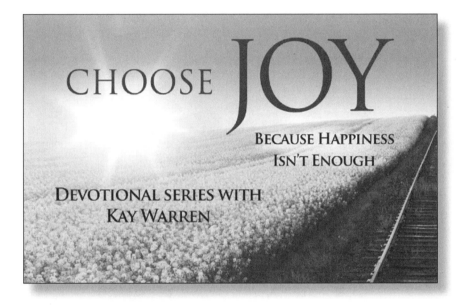

## Sign Up for Our Free 30-Day Devotional

Connect daily with Kay Warren through free CHOOSE JOY video devotions. For thirty days you'll receive an email from Kay, sharing the concepts from CHOOSE JOY in her warm, conversational style. She'll share not only her personal struggle to live a joyful life but also the truth that joy is available to anyone who seeks it.

Sign up today at
www.KayWarren.com/Devotions

## Stay Connected with Kay

www.KayWarren.com

Visit www.KayWarren.com to connect with other readers, sign up for the free email devotions, and order the *Choose Joy* curriculum. In addition, you will find information and resources about the passions of Kay's heart: orphans and vulnerable children, a Christian response to HIV and AIDS, the PEACE Plan, encouragement for pastors' wives, as well as current articles she has written.

## KAY WARREN App

Download the free iPhone or Android app titled "Kay Warren," where you will find video messages from Kay, helpful resources, and daily challenges to courageously choose joy in every part of your life.

## Facebook Fan Page
Join Kay's facebook community and "like" her fan page.

## Follow Kay on Twitter
Get encouragement and updates from Kay on Twitter: @KayWarren1

Visit www.KayWarren.com, email Kay@KayWarren.com, or call the office of Kay Warren at (949) 609-8552.